RECREATIONAL MUSIC MAKING HANDBOOK for Piano Teachers

Brian Chung & Brenda Dillon

*This book is dedicated to Karl Bruhn,
the father of Recreational Music Making,
whose lifelong dedication to the music making
community has been an inspiration to us all.*

ISBN-10: 0-7390-6120-8
ISBN-13: 978-0-7390-6120-6

FOREWORD

There are moments in history when the time is right for something really important to happen.

In the early 1960s, the doo-wop music of the fifties was getting stale and an emerging generation of young Americans—dubbed the "baby boomers"—was growing restless for change. When the Beatles (and a cadre of other British bands) landed on America's eastern shores, the "boomers" went wild. Almost overnight, the British invasion was rocking and rolling the nation from coast to coast. Sales of recorded music hit unprecedented heights. The baby boom generation triggered a cataclysmic shift in the musical landscape that would last for decades. The time was right, and a *movement* happened.

By the late 1970s, that same generation—now with children in tow—started buying homes to accommodate their growing families. Tending to be do-it-yourselfers, they began consuming tools, materials, and supplies by the boatload. It wasn't long before the gurus of retailing spotted a colossal opportunity, and a new kind of shopping format was born: the home improvement superstore. Within a decade, these stores were everywhere. Retail giants such as Home Depot and Lowe's didn't appear by accident; they were the natural byproduct of the baby boom. The time was right, and a *movement* happened.

Today, the baby boom generation is turning the corner on retirement. For many, the kids are grown, education expenses are subsiding, and schedules are less full. They can finally begin to explore the list of things they have always *wanted* to do. High on that list is music making. Surveys show that one of the greatest regrets among baby boomers is that they quit music lessons as children.[1] Today, tens of millions of boomers long to express themselves with an instrument, but just don't know how to get started. For music educators and purveyors of musical instruments, this represents an opportunity of massive proportions.

Once again, the time is right for something really important to happen.

This book can help prepare you for the next seismic shift of the baby boom generation as it redefines aging and retirement. The boomers will be offered many options for investing their considerable time and resources. In the coming decades, will they choose vacation time-shares, ocean cruises and golf? Or will they embrace the life changing power of music making?

The answer is up to you.

---

1 "U. S. Gallup Poll," *2008 Music USA NAMM Global Report* (August 2008), 139.

CONTENTS

INTRODUCTION TO RECREATIONAL MUSIC MAKING

Back in the late 1990s, Karl Bruhn and Remo Belli, both icons of the music products industry and noted visionaries, gazed into the future and saw something deeply compelling. Both men had been continually searching for trends that could affect the world of music making. Like other students of demography, they had watched with keen interest as the baby boomer generation journeyed through the stages of life and transformed society at every turn. Particularly intriguing to them were the following insights about baby boomers nearing retirement:

- They expect to live longer than any previous generation.

- They view *quality* of life in later years as more important than *quantity* (length) of life.

- Besides finances, they are concerned most about maintaining mental and physical health in retirement.

- Most have always wanted to play a musical instrument.[1]

Noting the concern for health, Bruhn wondered whether there might be a scientific connection between music making and improved mental and physical health. His interest led him to several researchers, one of whom was Barry Bittman, M.D., a prominent neurologist and wellness expert whose studies uncovered other relevant information:

- A significant number of doctor visits involve stress-related issues.[2]

- 40% of American workers consider their jobs very (or extremely) stressful.[3]

- Chronic stress can lead to a myriad of mental and physical ailments.

- A reduction of the impact of stress can positively affect one's well-being and quality of life.

Bittman's research showed that group-based music lessons—when not focused on performance or mastery—were found to improve mood states, reduce burnout and reverse the effects of stress at the genomic level.[4] Based on these findings, it is logical to surmise that active engagement in non-pressured music making could significantly improve quality of life and personal well being among all who would embrace it. This weighty premise became the basis for a new philosophy of music participation that Bruhn and Bittman dubbed "Recreational Music Making," or RMM.

1 "U. S. Gallup Poll," *2008 Music USA NAMM Global Report* (August 2008), 139.
2 Herbert Benson, M. D., Julie Corliss and Geoffrey Cowley, "Brain Check," *Newsweek* 144 (September 2004), 44–47.
3 Northwestern National Life Insurance Company, "Employee Burnout: Causes and Cures," (1992), quoted in Steven Sauter et al., "Stress...at Work," *NIOSH Publication 99–101*, http:www.cdc.gov/niosh/stresswk.html.
4 Barry Bittman et al., "Recreational music-making modulates the human stress response; a preliminary individualized gene expression strategy," *Medical Science Monitor* 11, no. 3 (2005), 31–40.

The implications of RMM are enormous for the music community. If widely accepted, it could be an answer to some of the major wellness issues facing an entire generation. Excited by the possibilities, Bruhn and Bittman presented RMM to the worldwide music products industry at the NAMM Global Summit in Estepona, Spain in 2002. They described it as "a new strategy for enabling people who never before considered themselves 'musical' to discover the joy and wellness benefits of playing a musical instrument." This marked the beginning of an emerging musical movement that is the subject of this book.

Recreational Music Making could be the fuel that launches a major resurgence of music making around the world—the platform that restores music making to its rightful place in our culture as an essential component of a healthy, balanced life. But, for teachers and music retailers who want to be part of its growth, many questions may arise:

- How does a teacher reach out to the baby boomers?
- What styles of music will they want to learn?
- Will they have the same musical goals as younger students?
- Will they want to achieve a high level of proficiency or just have fun?
- Can they be taught with the same materials and methodology used to teach children?
- Will they want to learn individually or in groups?
- Could RMM persuade younger dropouts to keep playing music?
- What are the attributes of a great RMM teacher?

This book was written to answer these questions. May it help you to cultivate a world filled with music makers.

Chapter 1 THE PHILOSOPHY OF RECREATIONAL MUSIC MAKING

Picture this scenario. One hundred people are chosen at random and placed in a room. They are asked the following question, "Would you like to be the next Lang Lang?" Those who answer *yes* are invited to stay. Those who say *no* are asked to leave.

Eighty-five people leave. Exit surveys reveal that very few knew what a "Lang Lang" was. Some respondents, particularly older adults, left because they thought he or she might be a rap artist. Several others couldn't comprehend why any human being would want to be a panda.

Fifteen remain. When told that Lang Lang is a renowned concert pianist from China, five young people, disappointed that he was *not* an emerging rap artist, quickly depart. Another five who thought he was a Chinese basketball star follow suit.

Only five remain. These persons say that playing music is important to them. But when told how many years of diligent study and practice would be required to become a concert pianist of Lang Lang's stature, three more leave the room.

Two are left. When interviewed, both say they are studying classical piano and aspire to be accomplished players, but are unsure about their chances of becoming a concert artist. When told how few pianists actually find careers on the concert stage, one of them declares that she will always love the piano, but would rather use her talents to become a doctor.

One person remains…wondering silently whether the dream is worth the cost.

Not everyone wants to be the next Lang Lang. Yet, much of the music teaching profession is designed with that destination in mind. Many college and university music programs are geared to produce high achievement in performance, or to produce future teachers who will emphasize high achievement in performance among their students. Many independent teaching studios are oriented in the same way. The primary goal is to nurture the talented students who will excel.

This, by itself, is a worthy objective. In the story above, the few who stayed in the room until the end are certainly deserving of careful attention and nurture. But what about the vast majority of people who left? Some will participate in music making at varying levels throughout their lives. But most—perhaps over 90%—may *never* have a connection with the piano or any other musical instrument. Is this acceptable? Should they be ignored? Are they irrelevant to the future of music making?

By focusing only on the few who have obvious musical ability, has the music teaching profession inadvertently helped to create a society in which most people believe they lack the talent and skills to participate?

Could the benign neglect of this unskilled majority be one reason why so many millions ignore "serious" music making…and why it struggles to gain the respect and prominence it deserves in today's culture? If so, what can anyone do about it?

Recreational Music Making (RMM) was created to address these questions. It was founded upon the following core principles:

- All people should experience the joy and benefits of music making.
- Music making can be enjoyed without stress and performance requirements.
- Music making can nurture the *whole* person and improve quality of life.
- Music making is beneficial to the health of the participant.

Within this framework, anyone can find success in making music. Millions who have been intimidated by performance standards will have "permission" to participate at their own level of comfort and enjoyment. Those same millions, no longer on the sidelines wishing they could play but now actively engaged in music making, could become passionate advocates for an art form that needs all the support it can get.

Teachers, too, can benefit from RMM. In addition to the financial rewards from teaching adult group lessons at times of the day when traditional students are in school, teachers will experience less stress in RMM teaching because:

- Classes and voluntary performance events are low-stress for students, creating a more relaxed atmosphere for the teacher.
- Diligent student practice, often a frustrating motivational problem for teachers and parents, is encouraged but not required for success.
- The non-competitive group lesson experience (in which class members encourage and support one another) helps reduce the dropout rate and the pressure on the teacher to single-handedly keep students playing.

RMM can become a key component of a healthy, balanced experience for the teacher as well as the student. One can simply relax and have fun introducing people to the love of music making.

So, how does RMM instruction differ from traditional teaching? Chapter 2 will explain.

Chapter 2 TRADITIONAL VERSUS RECREATIONAL TEACHING

Barbara C. has run a private piano studio for the past 18 years. She loves her work and her students, but can't help but notice that many things have changed. Her students, who were always distracted by extra-curricular activities at school, now spend additional hours each day sending messages and updating their profiles through online networks. Video games, which had become less intrusive in recent years, have roared back with a vengeance—stealing precious hours with new games that simulate real-life activities with amazing accuracy.

Her students seem less focused. They're practicing less, and it shows in their playing. Barbara feels the increasing stress of trying to satisfy parental expectations despite decreasing student commitment. She tries to shrug off feelings of disappointment and failure when students—especially the talented ones—quit lessons to concentrate on other pursuits. Reflecting on all these changes, Barbara confesses that piano teaching just isn't what it used to be.

These are the struggles that afflict many piano teachers in today's hectic world. Forced to compete with an ever-growing list of alternative choices, they have grown frustrated—weary of fighting a constant battle against everything else that vies for students' time. Much of this pressure and frustration is brought on by the requirements of traditional teaching, requirements that set high expectations for both student and teacher.

Although definitions of traditional teaching may vary widely, the following attributes provide a general description. In traditional piano teaching:

- Primary emphasis is placed on achieving a high level of performance.
- A structured curriculum is employed.
- Teaching occurs primarily through private/individual lessons.
- The teacher prescribes the direction and style of the lesson.
- The teacher appraises the student's level of success.

This is a good methodology that continues to serve the needs of many aspiring and accomplished musicians today. However, it fails to meet the needs of millions of potential music makers who find the traditional learning style too solitary or who cannot live up to its standards of achievement.

As a worthy alternative, RMM teaching holds the promise of creating millions of *new* music makers who could not only transform the music teaching profession, but also elevate the importance and impact of music making in our culture. RMM teaching can be described by the following attributes:

- Performance is not emphasized or required.
- The curriculum can bend and adapt at any time.
- Teaching occurs primarily in *group* lessons.
- The student and teacher participate *together* in prescribing the direction/style of lessons.
- Students learn from the teacher *and* other class members.
- The *student* appraises the level of success.

RMM teaching is, above all, designed to be fun and social. It makes music making accessible for anyone, and puts as its first priority the needs and desires of the student.

CONTRASTING THE PHILOSOPHIES (of Traditional and RMM Teaching)

While traditional teaching is oriented toward school-age students, RMM is designed primarily for adult learners and addresses one of the deepest regrets expressed by adults: the fact that they gave up music lessons as children.

Traditional teaching is usually offered during limited after-school hours. RMM classes can be taught during the day (particularly for retired adults). This offers the teacher more flexible hours and the potential for additional income.

While traditional teaching is continually focused on advancement to the next level, RMM allows students to find *their own level of achievement*. Adult learners aren't striving to become the next Vladimir Horowitz; they simply want to attain a reasonable level of skill that allows them to play many of their favorite songs.

In traditional teaching, not every student will succeed. Students who fail to advance are sometimes encouraged to pursue other avenues of expression. In RMM teaching, *all* students succeed. Since the students participate in crafting the curriculum, they can establish attainable goals that will ensure success.

In traditional teaching, the teacher is the primary provider of encouragement and accountability. In RMM teaching, fellow class members play an equal role with the teacher in encouraging progress. Often, social interaction with classmates will become as important as the music itself. Students will progress not because the curriculum demands it, but because they enjoy the process of learning with others.

As stated in Chapter 1, traditional teaching can be stressful for both teacher and student with its emphasis on performance. RMM teaching is far less stressful. Since high-level performance is never required, students can enjoy the playing experience in groups without pressure and anxiety. Solo playing is always voluntary.

SIMILARITIES SHARED BY TRADITIONAL AND RMM TEACHING

Note Reading and Repertoire

Like the students of traditional teaching, RMM students will play a diverse repertoire and learn how to read music—for some, the entire grand staff; for others, only the right hand of a lead sheet. During the final class of each multi-week session, the teacher will suggest a range of musical repertoire appropriate for the skill level of a class (e.g. classical themes, Broadway/movie hits, popular songs, jazz classics, holiday music, patriotic melodies) and allow class members to vote on the book or books that will be used for the next session. Students will learn note reading in their chosen style.

Technique

As in traditional lessons, RMM students *do* learn proper technique. While traditional students learn this from the teacher, RMM students will often be influenced most by the improving technique of classmates. Class members watch one another and are guided by those whom the teacher praises as role models.

Performance

While solo performance is never required, a majority of RMM students *do* want to perform for their class, and eventually in more public settings. However, such performances will always be at the student's discretion. Enrollment in RMM classes will be maximized when students are told in advance that they won't have to perform unless they choose to do so.

CHARACTERISTICS OF THE BEST RMM TEACHERS

- They are genuinely concerned about helping people live quality lives.
- They value the whole person, not just the music.
- They are willing to put the students' goals and preferences ahead of their own.
- They see themselves more as "facilitators of learning" than teachers.
- They are willing to let students move at their own pace.
- They enjoy smiling, laughing and having fun.

Having outlined the RMM philosophy and the comparisons with traditional teaching, the following chapters will explore the "nuts and bolts" of RMM teaching.

"RMM teaching is the most rewarding of my entire career. I feel as though I have found my calling—a way to give back."

—RMM Teacher

Chapter Three GETTING STARTED

John S. received his bachelor's degree in music two years ago and is now a full-time piano teacher in a small town. He has a private studio with 18 students that keeps him fairly busy. With plans to marry next year, however, he needs to increase his income.

John heard something about "RMM adult teaching" at a music conference and thinks it might be a good way for him to teach during daytime hours when his current students are in school. He remembers studying some group piano concepts during his pedagogy classes in college, but he wasn't very interested at the time. Plus, that instruction was geared toward younger students rather than adults. Now, he has many questions...and isn't quite sure how to get started.

The next two chapters were designed for John. They will provide answers to a range of practical questions that any new RMM teacher might ask, including:

- Where should I teach?
- What instruments should be available?
- What ages should I teach?
- How much should I charge?
- What materials should be used?
- What replaces recitals?
- How can I partner with a retailer (if I'm not teaching in a store)?

The following answers will provide a solid framework for building a successful RMM program.

WHERE SHOULD I TEACH?

Teachers who have sufficient space for group lessons in their home studio will probably decide to teach RMM at home. But for others with smaller studios, group lessons can present a challenge. Fortunately, there are many alternatives. RMM can be taught in a variety of other venues—music stores, senior centers, places of worship, retirement communities, community/recreation centers, schools, colleges and universities to name just a few. Each of these locations has pros and cons, some of which are listed below.

Home Studios

Teaching in a home studio is convenient and provides complete independence for the teacher. However, the size of the studio can be an issue, as it may limit the number of people who can participate. There may also be parking and zoning issues. Still, the home studio may be the easiest first step for a new RMM teacher.

Retail Music Stores

Music stores can be ideal locations for RMM teaching. Most retailers are happy to accommodate teaching programs that can help create future customers for their store. If they have confidence in a teacher's desire and ability to create more music makers, they will often partner with that teacher to make RMM classes possible.

12

Many piano stores have a dedicated space for group lessons that contains either a piano lab (typically 4–8 digital pianos) or multiple acoustic pianos that can accommodate group lessons. There are usually no parking or zoning issues. The teacher may lose some independence having to adapt to any protocols or requirements of the store's teaching program. But when a retail store is supportive and cooperative, there is no better place to conduct RMM classes.

If the music store does not have dedicated space for the teaching program, it is best to search for another venue. Teachers may find it difficult to conduct classes on the showroom floor with customers coming in and out and phones ringing.

Also, to avoid future complications the storeowner (or education director) should clearly identify which pianos will remain in the teaching space throughout the RMM session. When the number and models of pianos change from week to week (as instruments are sold and moved), the flow of teaching can be disrupted. Know in advance how frequently these changes will occur and incorporate this information into the decision process.

Colleges and Universities

Colleges and universities can also be good RMM venues. Like music stores, they often have piano labs or dedicated rooms with multiple pianos. There can be some complications, however, including: finding available rooms at desired times, finding parking on busy campuses, and having to conform to university/college requirements for teaching programs. Circumstances will vary widely from school to school; so one shouldn't give up if the first school approached is not a good fit. Many community colleges have a strong desire to reach out to adult students and may welcome RMM classes on their campuses.

Retirement Communities

Retirement communities are perfect sites for RMM teaching, since they regularly host learning activities for adults. Although they typically have only one acoustic piano, this obstacle has an easy solution that will be covered later in this chapter.

Retirement communities offer large concentrations of fairly affluent senior adults who want to stay active and engaged with other people. Accordingly, they represent an outstanding fit for RMM teaching and should be considered by every teacher. The only drawback might be the "static" nature of their clientele. Residents tend to move infrequently, and new people arrive only when vacancies become available. So, while the sheer size of retirement communities makes them irresistible candidates for RMM classes, know that some communities may not offer strong potential for long-term growth after the existing population has been reached.

Senior and Recreation Centers

Senior centers and recreation centers can offer a more diverse and varying clientele than retirement communities, and may provide greater potential for student prospects and stronger long-term growth. These centers typically provide an array of courses and activities that are offered at moderate to low cost. They advertise regularly with catalogs and/or newsletter mailings that can help significantly with RMM recruiting. The only drawback may be financial. Since many visitors may be living on lower or fixed incomes, a teacher may have to reduce session fees to remain competitive with other course offerings. Still, senior centers and recreation centers represent exceptional opportunities for the aspiring RMM teacher.

Places of Worship

Places of worship are also excellent venues for RMM teaching. In particular, churches tend to own many pianos—though the instruments are rarely in the same room. Quite often, choir directors, excited by the prospect of having new choir members who can read music, will not only arrange to have multiple pianos placed in one room, but also assist with recruiting for RMM classes. Be sure to explain the sight-reading benefits of RMM to the choir director to maximize the chances of securing an appropriate location.

Also note that some church staff members will see RMM classes as a ministry opportunity to engage adults in the wider community who do not normally attend their church. RMM can serve as an outreach to "shut-ins" and seniors, or a chance for adult church members to build relationships with friends or business colleagues who wouldn't otherwise visit a church setting. Be sure to mention the potential ministry value of RMM when discussing the concept with the church staff.

Summary of Venues

This is only a partial list of possible locations for RMM classes. Since every community is different, be creative. There may be other ideal locations that are unique to one's own area. It should be kept in mind that an RMM teacher may need to approach several different venues before finding the optimal situation. Some teachers, having found several favorable venues, may develop successful RMM classes on separate days in many different locations.

WHAT INSTRUMENTS SHOULD BE AVAILABLE?

Group lessons require at least two pianos. When a venue has only one, teachers can find several low-cost solutions for a second instrument. Some purchase affordable digital pianos that are light enough to carry into the teaching location. Others contact a local piano retailer to discuss loan/rent/purchase programs. As mentioned earlier, most retailers will be happy to partner with teaching programs that can create future customers for their store.

Types of Instruments

Much of the success of RMM classes is dependent on the quality of keyboard instruments available for teaching. Sub-standard instruments can sometimes produce disappointing experiences. It is important for classroom instruments to be tuned and in good working order. When this is not possible, find another location or build a partnership with a piano retailer to secure better instruments.

Similarly, poor-quality practice instruments at home can cause discouragement for a student. RMM teachers should stress that students *do* need an acceptable home practice instrument to make the most of their RMM experience. Acoustic pianos and keyboards with full-size, weighted keys are preferable to small portable keyboards. If students do not have an acceptable instrument at home, they may be guided toward a retailer that has a rent/purchase plan.

WHAT AGES SHOULD I TEACH?

RMM is an effective way to introduce people of *all* ages to the joys of music making. It was created to provide an alternative pathway for anyone who has been discouraged or intimidated by the performance-based approach. Although adults have been the primary focus of RMM since its inception, teachers should realize that *RMM is not age specific.*

For teachers who prefer working with children, RMM may be the perfect solution to reduce the dropout rate. Children who can't seem to thrive in the traditional system could elect to join an RMM group class where enjoyment is emphasized over performance. Teenagers who lack the time to embrace formal training could still engage in music making through RMM.

But because the adult market represents such an immense opportunity for the musical community (as discussed in the Foreword), *teachers are encouraged to begin RMM classes with adults*—particularly baby boomers. This demographic group must be attracted to music making *now*, before they choose other ways to spend their time and resources. And while children have many avenues of musical instruction available to them, adults have few such programs tailored to their specific musical aspirations. RMM fills a void in the adult segment and offers the piano teaching profession a unique opportunity—one that should not be ignored.

Ages and Venues

The venue selected for RMM teaching will often dictate the ages of students who enroll.

- Senior centers and retirement communities will typically reach an older crowd. Some programs will specify "55 and older" for activities, but will usually accept participants who are younger. Strive to be inclusive whenever possible.

- College and university classes can attract students of multiple ages, from college students to "50-somethings." Seniors may avoid these venues due to parking issues and a reluctance to attend classes in the evening.

- Music stores, places of worship and home studios can attract a wide range of ages depending on the time of the day classes are taught. Retired adults and mothers of young children prefer daytime classes. Working professionals prefer evening classes because of work schedules.

Keep in mind that older adult learners can sometimes be intimidated by teenagers, so avoid mixing these two age groups (unless you're certain they can get along well).

People in all of these age groups have a common desire to learn to play the piano in a non-stressful environment. Teachers should decide which demographic groups are the best fit for their personality and teaching style and select venues (and music) that will best attract and retain people from those groups.

HOW MUCH SHOULD I CHARGE?

The answer to this question depends on several factors, including *where* you teach, *whom* you teach and what other teachers in the area are charging.

Where You Teach

Some regions of the country have a higher cost-of-living than others. Lesson fees should reflect those differences. For example, a session taught in New York City or Boston might be twice the cost of an identical session taught in a small rural town.

Whom You Teach

When the majority of enrolled students are retired and living on modest fixed incomes, fees might be considerably lower than the fees one might charge in an affluent retirement community. This may seem unfair, but consumers understand that costs of goods and services will vary from place to place. (Ask anyone who has ever purchased food at an airport.)

What Other Teachers Are Charging

Begin by asking parents of piano students in the local area what they pay for lessons. This survey will provide an "average local cost" that will be helpful in calculating an appropriate fee for RMM classes.

How to Charge

RMM teachers generally charge by the month or by the complete session rather than per class. Most teachers charge in advance for an entire session to minimize bookkeeping.

What to Charge

A good rule of thumb for setting session fees is to estimate the average cost of *one half-hour private* lesson in the area and multiply that figure by the number of RMM classes in a session.

For example, suppose an average half-hour private lesson in the local area costs $15.00. Using the above formula, the cost of an 8-week RMM session would be $15.00 times eight sessions—or *$120.00* per student.

A survey of RMM teachers across the U.S. showed that fees vary widely, from $40.00 to $200.00 for eight weeks of lessons ($110.00 average). Some fees include materials, while others do not. The fee per student should remain the same no matter how many students are in a class, which is why RMM classes can be quite lucrative for a teacher.

WHAT MATERIALS SHOULD BE USED?

RMM students typically enroll in piano classes because they want to accomplish two things:

1. Play a favorite piece of music. Choices may be as diverse as *Für Elise, Music Box Dancer,* a classic hymn, a Beatles oldie, a Broadway hit, a movie theme or a current radio tune.
2. Understand how to play chords. Chords are the harmonic basis for all music and are fascinating to early learners.

The best RMM materials help students accomplish these two primary goals as quickly as possible. The faster that RMM students can play the melody and chords of their favorite songs, the more enthusiastic they will be. Materials that include CD or MIDI accompaniments to help simple melodies sound spectacular are even more valuable to early RMM learners.

Based on feedback from RMM students, the best beginner course materials have the following attributes:

- Familiar music.
- Easy-to-read font and note sizes.
- Pages that are not too crowded.
- Brief and concise explanations of music fundamentals that contain essential information only.
- Accompaniments provided at slower tempos for learning and slightly faster for normal playing.

- Separation of hands at the beginning, followed by simple pieces that allow hands to play together.
- Simple chords, introduced fairly early in the process.
- Lead sheets—chords with single-note melodies—utilized as important song-learning tools.
- A glossary of musical terms and symbols.

RMM students with advancing skills appreciate different curricula, involving:

- A mix of familiar music and new, unfamiliar music.
- A wider range of styles, including classical, popular, hymns, jazz, etc.
- Some music theory, with focus on how it might speed up the learning process.
- More advanced lead sheets with accompaniment styles.
- Ideas for making written pieces more colorful and interesting, such as alternative chords and various accompaniment styles.
- Traditional technical training, including scales, arpeggios and exercises.
- An introduction to jazz improvisation—especially the blues.

Most publishers have music and curricula that address these requirements and preferences.

RMM teachers should always be listening to class members to determine what materials can best keep students inspired and engaged. Give students a range of options and let them choose materials that the majority of the class will enjoy. Groups that take ownership of their music and direction are usually the ones that continue learning together.

WHAT REPLACES RECITALS?

To some people, playing in a piano recital is the musical equivalent of having dental surgery. They cringe with apprehension at the very thought of the experience. Why does this happen? It's because recitals dictate a mandatory time to perform—whether or not the performer is ready. Many people are not as afraid of *playing* as they are of *not being ready* to play. When one doesn't feel ready (or truly isn't prepared), mistakes and meltdowns can happen, and embarrassment follows.

RMM solves this problem with a cardinal rule—*all solo playing is voluntary.* That is, "You play only when you're ready." The reality is that most students really *do* want to perform for their friends and family. They just want to do it on their own terms and in their own time. With this in mind, RMM teachers have replaced traditional recitals with new types of events, three of which are described below:

The Piano Party

The Piano Party is a casual event held in someone's home or in the teacher's studio. RMM students gather for a casual evening of food, fun and friendship. Anyone who feels ready to play a piece simply sits at the piano and plays. When the player is finished, everyone cheers. It's a relaxed, informal setting to perform (or not perform) among friends. The Piano Party involves little stress and requires minimal preparation for the teacher.

The RMM Player's Club

The RMM Player's Club is a periodic event (usually held in a music store) that allows the RMM teacher to present special material or topics that would not ordinarily be part of RMM classes. For example, a teacher might demonstrate how to record a piece on a digital piano or bring in a guest artist to perform and interact with students. At every "Club Nite," students can volunteer to play solos and duets for their classmates. It's a fun, relaxed way to let RMM students perform in a safe and encouraging environment.

The Piano Celebration

Start with the key elements of a traditional recital (a large space and a big audience), add plenty of food, remove *all* stress, and *voilà*—you've got a Piano Celebration.[1] This event brings RMM students together with their friends, family and co-workers for an evening of musical merriment.

A celebration can take the form of a themed dinner, a "wine and cheese" party, a dessert social, or any other format that makes the evening festive. RMM students can design special invitations to send to friends and loved ones. The bigger the audience the better, since everyone who attends a celebration is a candidate to become a future RMM student.

Although a special guest performer can enhance the proceedings, the true highlight of the evening is the *background music* provided by the RMM students themselves. In keeping with the RMM philosophy, there is no schedule, no applause and no pressure. Students simply play when they're ready. And though there is no applause, all the performers will know that they were heard and appreciated. With this concept, the goals of a conventional recital are met—without the associated angst.

Of course, an event of this kind requires ample space and well-prepared instruments, which illustrates one of many reasons why a partnership with a local retailer is beneficial for every RMM teacher.

HOW CAN I PARTNER WITH A RETAILER (If I'm Not Teaching in a Store)?

Teachers who don't teach RMM classes in music stores have still found it highly advantageous to join forces with an area piano retailer. Teachers and retailers can be excellent partners when both are focused on creating *more music makers*. RMM programs enjoy their greatest success when teachers and retailers are working together toward this goal.

Most piano retailers understand that they can benefit greatly by working with teachers who know how to build and expand an RMM program. Many retailers have no teaching programs of their own and rely on the teaching community to generate future customers. Therefore, teachers should know that most piano retailers are genuinely interested in becoming partners in RMM by providing resources that may include facilities for group events, loaned or reduced-price instruments, program advertising or other valuable support. *(See Chapter 9 for further information on this topic.)*

---

1 The authors wish to acknowledge Debra and Matt Perez, owners of two piano stores in South Texas, for originating the concept of a piano celebration.

At the same time, teachers must understand that such a partnership must be *mutually* beneficial. That is, retailers must accrue tangible benefits from their support of a teacher's RMM program. Such benefits are critical to a retailer's success and survival. Some ideas for providing benefits to a retailer:

- With each beginning class, stress the need for students to have an acceptable practice instrument at home. Recommend the partnering retailer as the "store of choice" for instrument rental or purchase by students.

- Plan group activities at the retailer's store at least every other month, if possible. Some RMM programs have an RMM Player's Club that meets in the store and gives students exposure to an array of quality instruments. Include the retailer in the planning of such events so that the students can get to know the storeowner and the sales staff. Encourage students to play various instruments whenever they visit the store.

- Since many storeowners and staff salespersons play the piano, ask them to give playing demonstrations during RMM Player's Club events. This involvement will give the store staff greater credibility during the piano sales process. The Player's Club is not designed to be a sales event, but such demonstrations can help to "plant seeds" for future purchases.

- A retailer will typically assign a member of the sales staff to serve as the host of each Player's Club meeting. Invite that staff member to join the class for lunch or any after-class gathering that may be planned. This will provide a great opportunity for that staff person to interact with students on a social basis.

- Encourage students to attend concerts in the retailer's store when a guest artist performs. When possible, ask the artist to hold a special question/answer session for RMM class members after the performance. Such learning opportunities are valuable for students and help to deepen their relationship with the store.

- If the retailer has a print music department, ask the department manager to give students a tour of the area so that they can easily find the music they want to play. After placing a music order for a class, encourage students to pick up their music at the store. This will provide another opportunity for students to bond with the store and see the breadth of music and accessories (such as metronomes and flash cards) available to them.

Teachers need students to survive in the profession. Similarly, retailers need customers to survive in business and continue to serve the community. When both parties are working together on behalf of students, the outcome will always be "win-win" for everyone involved. *(See Chapter 9 for additional insight into the benefits of a symbiotic relationship between teacher and retailer.)*

Having covered many of the foundational questions about RMM teaching in this chapter, Chapter 4 will discuss the next steps required to make the first RMM class a reality.

Chapter 4 NEXT STEPS

Mary T. feels she has acquired a pretty good understanding of the RMM philosophy. She knows what it is, why it exists, where it can be taught and whom she wants to reach. But to turn the concept into reality, she needs answers to many questions that begin with "how." Since her home studio is too small for group classes, how should she approach the possible outside locations for RMM classes? How can she recruit adult students? How should the classes be organized? How should she prepare for the first class? Mary is ready to dive in, but wishes she could talk with a teacher who has done this before.

For the teacher who feels like Mary, this chapter will provide answers to the critical "how to" questions that can help to get an RMM program started.

HOW TO APPROACH AN OUTSIDE FACILITY

After identifying one or more favorable locations for RMM classes, schedule a meeting with the persons who direct or coordinate programs for these venues. Be prepared to cover the following list of topics during a meeting:

What is Recreational Music Making?

The Introduction and Chapter 1 of this handbook will be useful in answering this question. If the facility has a DVD player, show the 10-minute "RMM Documentary DVD" available from the National Piano Foundation (NPF). The DVD can be purchased from NPF for a nominal fee or viewed online at the NPF website, www.pianonet.com.

Why would an RMM piano class be beneficial to the facility?

The following talking points will be helpful:

- Most adults wish they could play music.
- Music making can reduce stress and improve health.

For churches:

- RMM can produce sight-readers for the choir.
- RMM can be an outreach to adults in the community-at-large.

For music retailers:

- RMM will build repeat traffic in the store.
- RMM will create future customers.

For retirement communities and senior centers:

- RMM is a valuable social networking activity for seniors.
- Music making engages the mind and body in healthful ways.

If, after discussing the above benefits, the program director agrees that RMM teaching would be valuable and appropriate for the facility, ask the following questions.

What instruments are currently available at the location?

Play all available instruments to see which ones are in satisfactory condition. The quality and number of available instruments will generally determine the format used for class sessions. Be sure to ask whether the facility would be willing to have the pianos tuned prior to the start of classes (four times per year is ideal).

Where in the facility could classes be taught?

If the director suggests a specific room, visit that room to answer several questions:

- Is the room large enough for a group class?
- If the room is located on an upper floor, is there elevator access for seniors?
- Does the room have satisfactory instruments? If not, can better instruments be brought in from other rooms?
- If another room has better instruments, could that room be used?
- If the teacher provides additional instruments for the room, can those instruments be safely stored in the room between classes?
- Will other classes or activities use the room? (This lets the teacher know whether extra prep time is required to "reset" the room before each class.)

Who will take responsibility for advertising and recruiting?

Some facilities (notably senior centers, recreation centers, and colleges) will take responsibility for attracting students through their catalogs and newsletters. Music stores and churches will often help with advertising in flyers and bulletins, but will expect the teacher to do most of the recruiting.

Who will contact the students to schedule classes?

Facilities that recruit students through catalogs and newsletters will normally inform enrolled students of class times without requiring assistance from the teacher. When the teacher is the primary recruiter, it is usually the teacher's responsibility to announce the class schedule to enrolled students by mail, phone or e-mail.

Who will collect the fees?

Some venues will require that all fees be paid directly to the facility. Others will prefer to leave the bookkeeping to the teacher. Be sure this issue is clarified before classes are offered.

How will teacher pay be determined?

Some venues will let the teacher keep all lesson fees. Others will retain a portion of the tuition as a facility fee. This is a critical question that will help determine the financial viability of RMM classes in any venue. Be sure to clarify this issue before finalizing any agreement with a venue.

Will the teacher or the facility determine the curriculum?

Normally, the teacher will plan the curriculum. However, some music stores and colleges may have specific course requirements that must be followed to maintain consistency with their existing education programs. In these cases, the teacher must adjust the curriculum accordingly to meet the requirements of the facility.

When can classes be taught?

Determine what days and times are appropriate for RMM classes in the desired venue. If the venue promotes classes and activities with a catalog or newsletter, find out when the next mailing is planned. The date of the mailing may determine how soon classes can begin.

THE COURSE DESCRIPTION

When venues publish catalogs of course offerings, the teacher is often asked to draft a course description similar to other descriptions in the catalog. The following examples may be helpful:

PIANO FUN (BEGINNER)

Learn to play the piano in a relaxed atmosphere while having fun making music. Class is for beginners or those who have forgotten how to play. No experience necessary. Class size is limited. A book fee is to be paid to the instructor.

Time: Monday, 11:00 A.M.   Instructor: Mary Thomas

Although a teacher may want to offer other classes in addition to the beginning class, it is best to offer only a beginning class first. Once that class is a success, other classes will follow. Below are examples of higher-level course descriptions:

PIANO FUN (EARLY LEVEL I)

Reinforce concepts learned in the beginner class and continue to gain new skills that are helpful in learning early level music. The emphasis is on fun and personal enjoyment. Class size is limited.

PIANO FUN (EARLY LEVEL II)

Reinforce basic concepts of playing the piano and music reading. Continue to gain skills that are helpful in learning early level music. The emphasis is on fun and personal enjoyment. Class size is limited.

PIANO FUN (INTERMEDIATE)

Gain piano skills that are helpful in learning intermediate level music. In addition to learning new pieces of music, the class will develop technical skills and introduce theoretical information that will deepen the student's appreciation for music. Emphasis is on fun and personal enjoyment. Class size is limited.

PIANO FUN (ADVANCED)

Gain piano skills that are useful in learning advanced level music. In addition to learning new pieces of music, the class will delve deeper into the technical skills and theoretical information that will deepen the student's appreciation and love for music. Emphasis is on fun and personal enjoyment. Class size is limited.

In the last two course descriptions, the words *intermediate* and *advanced* are used only to describe music that is progressively more challenging. The seasoned teacher should note that the music played at these levels might not be classified as *intermediate* and *advanced* in the traditional curriculum. In fact, an *advanced* piece for an RMM student might be classified as *early intermediate* in the traditional sense.

The longer students continue in RMM classes, the more challenging the music can become. However, this advancement must be at the *student's* discretion. Some will choose to plateau at a certain skill level and simply learn more songs at that level. Others will desire to learn more difficult music on a continuing basis (or even move into private lessons). In RMM teaching, either direction is acceptable. The goal of the RMM teacher is to keep students playing music at the level of their choice.

HOW TO RECRUIT STUDENTS

The following list, compiled by successful RMM teachers, describes ways to recruit students:

- Ask current students (both private and group) to recommend the RMM class to others.
- Speak personally with parents and grandparents of current school-age students and invite them to join an RMM class, or send an RMM invitation flyer home with students.
- Contact local church choir directors and present RMM classes as a way to promote sight-reading skills among current and prospective choir members.
- Write articles about RMM classes for the local paper.
- Write articles about RMM classes for newsletters circulated by senior centers and retirement communities.
- Announce and promote a series of "demonstration lessons" at selected venues.
- Ask a regular piano technician—especially one to whom you refer students—to distribute RMM flyers to piano clients.
- Ask a supportive music retailer to distribute RMM invitation flyers to customers and display RMM posters in the store.
- Place RMM flyers on bulletin boards of non-music locations frequented by adults (e.g. coffee shops, grocery stores, etc.)
- Include RMM class information in church bulletins, bulletin boards and newsletters.
- Post RMM class information on networking websites such as Facebook and Craigslist.
- Post RMM class information on your own home studio website.
- Send press releases to newspapers and radio stations with a public service announcement about RMM classes for adults.
- Present demonstration classes at senior fairs, health events, malls, etc.

Independent RMM teachers have found that paid advertising is not very effective for recruiting students. It is costly and often gets buried in a sea of other advertisements.

Creating a Flyer

The following sample advertisement contains several key elements that should be included in any RMM promotional piece:

- A headline with accompanying subtext that gives hope of success to those who have always wanted to play the piano.

- A photo of people having fun at the instrument. If there is sufficient space, include several photos showing various age groups participating. Photos should feature people who represent the specific demographic group you want to attract.

- Words or phrases that describe attributes of the learning environment—including fun, freedom from stress, health/wellness benefits and the opportunity to make new friends.

- A specific call to action. In this example, the call to action is an invitation to attend a preview lesson. The phrase "class size is limited" may help to create a sense of urgency. Be sure the ad states clearly what you want the reader to do and how the reader should respond.

(See page 49 for full-size example.)

Spreading the Word

In contrast to paid advertising, the most effective promotion occurs by word of mouth. Once a successful RMM session is taught and students show their enthusiasm by enrolling in another session, the word will begin to spread quickly. Nothing is more powerful than the personal endorsement of students who are enjoying the RMM learning experience and are pleased with their progress. Using important recruiting words such as "fun," "fulfilling," and "non-stressful," they will tell friends, relatives, co-workers and acquaintances about the program. When this begins to happen, program growth is sure to follow.

The Ambassador Program

One idea for boosting enrollment is to give the most enthusiastic students the title of "RMM Ambassador." These Ambassadors would earn points (similar to frequent flyer points) for every new student they help enlist into classes. The teacher or the music store would track the points earned. Ambassadors could redeem these points for printed music, accessories or credit toward future class sessions.

Example:

Teacher Mary T. offers 50 "friendship points" to her ambassadors for every new friend (student) they enlist. At the beginning of the term, Mary gives ambassadors a list of gift items that could be redeemed for friendship points (e.g. sheet music is 15 points, themed music books are 50 points, a metronome is 200 points, free tuition to the next class session is 300 points). Generally, 50 friendship points is equal to $20 in merchandise.

Rick J., one of Mary's most excited ambassadors, helped bring in three new students this fall. He earned 150 friendship points that were used to get three music books. Now, Rick is hoping to get four more of his friends into RMM classes so he can get a metronome.

Excited students are the RMM teacher's most valuable asset and strongest form of advertising. As they thrive, so will any RMM program.

HOW TO ORGANIZE CLASSES

There are four key elements of an RMM class format—class size, class length, session length (number of classes per session), and make-up classes.

Class Size

Class size is determined by the number of available instruments and the comfort level of the teacher.

- **Two Pianos**—Teachers who have no access to a piano lab and are limited to two pianos may prefer a smaller class of 4–6 adults. This may be ideal for teachers who are uncomfortable with larger groups. Smaller class sizes are often better for beginning classes. As classes become more advanced, it is easy to increase to 6–10 students per class. Chapter 6 will describe how teachers can rotate people at the pianos to keep students engaged when they are away from the instruments.

- **Piano Labs**—In a piano lab setting, class size can vary according to the number of available instruments. There are typically 8–10 students per class depending on the teacher's comfort level in handling larger groups. The primary benefit of a lab setting is that it provides one keyboard for each student, thereby avoiding the need to rotate students across instruments. Chapter 7 will discuss the specifics of RMM lab teaching.

Class Length

The typical RMM class length is 60 minutes. When multiple classes are offered back-to-back, the teacher will normally shorten the class length to 50–55 minutes. This allows time for student transition and offers the opportunity for individual questions from students. Because adult RMM teaching doesn't require teacher interaction with parents after class, the transitions between classes are usually quite fluid and stress-free.

Session Length

The recommended session length is *eight* weeks, with one class per week. Experience has shown that adults may hesitate to make a longer commitment. Rather than sign up for a 10–12 week session, they are more likely to enroll in an 8-week program, enjoy the experience, and enroll in a subsequent 8-week session. The teacher can decide whether or not to provide a break between sessions depending on the teacher's schedule and the feedback of class members.

RMM classes taught at universities or colleges may follow a semester schedule, which can be 15–16 weeks. The longer term is usually not a problem in these venues, since it matches student expectations. Still, it is advisable to offer alternative 8-week sessions in other locations to accommodate students who won't (or can't) make a longer commitment.

Make-up Classes

Teachers who are new to RMM will be pleased to know that no make-up lessons are offered and no refunds given for missed classes. This information should be clearly communicated to students when they enroll. While new information will be presented each week, no single class session will provide skills or knowledge that cannot be learned in a subsequent session. Students who miss a class can make up lost ground by observing their classmates the following week. Often, students will help each other stay on track with the rest of the group. The camaraderie that develops among adults during RMM classes will be a delight for any teacher to observe.

Preparing for Subsequent Sessions

On the final class of the 8-week session, the teacher should play music from various books that are appropriate for the next skill level. Styles can include classical themes, Broadway/movie hits, popular songs, jazz classics, holiday music, and patriotic melodies to name a few. Class members should vote on the book or books they prefer for the next session. This gives class members a sense of ownership of the next session and increases the probability that they will enroll again.

Session Names

Some teachers use traditional titles for sessions such as *Beginner, Early Level I, Early Level II, Intermediate and Advanced.* This may be the best way to identify sessions if class members are demographically diverse and the personality of the group is determined and serious. Some groups will prefer these progress-related titles for their sessions.

In other situations, more colorful session titles can be used to boost camaraderie and enjoyment. After the beginner session, a teacher may invite the enrolled class members to select their own session title. Titles can be based on:

- The chosen music style, e.g. *Broadway's Best, All That Jazz,* or *Hooked on Classics.*
- The personality of class members, e.g. *Fast-Trackers.*
- Class demographics, e.g. *Forty-Somethings.*
- The time classes are taught, e.g. *One-O'Clock Wonders.*
- The day the class is taught, e.g. *Monday Madness.*

Titles can change with each new session. Or, if a group stays together and has a transferable title (such as *Monday Madness*), the title can remain over many sessions. In reality, however, the session titles aren't that important. Far more critical is student retention. The best session titles are ones that help to create interest, excitement or camaraderie—and that encourage students to keep learning.

Session Times

From the outset, be aware that class members will usually want a new session to be taught at the same time as their previous session. For example, if their beginner class was taught on Monday at 11:00 A.M., they will want their subsequent *Early Level I* class to be taught at that same time. This practice will boost re-enrollment. Plus, it will be much easier than trying to move a continuing class to a different hour or day.

As new sessions are offered, always try to keep class members together in the same time slot. Find a different time slot to start each new beginner class, keeping in mind that the new time slot may be occupied by a new, close-knit group of students for quite some time.

Should students be grouped according to their skill level?

Grouping students according to skill level offers the best situation for the students and the teacher. However, beginning classes won't always attract people with similar skills. Sometimes, student skill levels will vary widely from the first day. At other times, student skills will appear to be quite similar at the beginning but will diverge dramatically over the course of eight weeks. Neither of these situations is a problem in RMM teaching.

Some adults enroll as beginners because they took childhood lessons decades ago and have supposedly forgotten everything. Many of these students will be surprised how quickly their skills return. This rapid progress will not present a problem for the class as long as the teacher clarifies on the first day that the process will start from the very beginning. The teacher can assign extra music to these rapid learners or enlist them to help others who have had no prior training.

Other students may ask to repeat a level because they missed classes or were unable to practice sufficiently. This is perfectly acceptable (especially as the program expands to several levels) and represents the best way for students to find their own pace and grouping. Encourage students to move to the next level only when *they* believe they are ready.

Continually remind students that RMM is different from traditional higher education. There are no grades or credits required to graduate. In fact, graduation is never the destination. RMM classes are designed for students to continue learning and enjoying music making for a lifetime. Students may take a break from lessons or go on to other kinds of music making, but they should know they are always welcome to continue their RMM piano training.

HOW TO PREPARE FOR THE FIRST SESSION

Below is a checklist of items that should be accomplished before the first class meeting.

1. When possible, monitor enrollment and call students prior to the first class to introduce yourself and determine whether or not the students have enrolled in the appropriate class.

2. Select the book to use for the beginning class. A partial list of available materials can be found at www.RMMhandbook.com.

3. Prepare a student handout that confirms class dates, holidays (if any) and class guidelines regarding missed classes (i.e. no make-up classes or refunds for missed classes). In the handout, provide an e-mail address or telephone number that students can use to notify the teacher when absences occur.

4. Plan some reassuring words of welcome for the first day to remove any anxiety that students might be feel upon entering RMM classes. Some adults may have had less-than-favorable musical experiences as children and may be wondering whether this experience will be different. Establish a warm and inviting atmosphere by explaining the following:

   • Learning to play the piano does not require talent...only a desire to play.

   • The emphasis of RMM classes will be on having fun making music.

   • Solo playing will always be voluntary.

   • There will be no recitals!

   • Class members should come to class even when practice time has been minimal. Because solo playing is always voluntary, no one will ever be embarrassed by the lack of practice.

   • Class members will vote together on the books to be used in future 8-week sessions.

Having prepared fully for RMM classes, the teacher should now be ready to begin the first 8-week session. The next three chapters will offer ideas and concepts that can help make RMM groups successful once classes have begun.

"I no longer teach beginning adults in private lessons because they enjoy the group experience more and progress faster."

—RMM Teacher

Chapter 5 PRINCIPLES OF GROUP TEACHING

Jim D. is a recently retired chemical engineer who always wanted to play the piano. He started private lessons about two months ago, but was surprised to find the process so solitary. Compared with his weekly round of golf with engineering friends and his church bowling league on Tuesday nights, piano playing was downright lonely.

Jim mentioned this to his teacher, who suggested that he join an RMM class that she was starting on Thursday mornings. Jim enrolled in RMM and immediately loved the interaction with other students! He enjoyed the way everyone in the class supported and encouraged everyone else. He started bringing donuts to class and organized a big dinner for everyone when the session ended. Now, he's planning to bring his golfing buddies to RMM classes.

Jim admitted to his teacher that he was having second thoughts about playing the piano after several weeks of private lessons. But RMM classes have made all the difference. Jim now wants to be a lifelong music maker.

Many adults are like Jim. They want to be involved in activities that are both fun and social. They enjoy the camaraderie of others and want to learn and grow in "community." That's why most RMM teaching is done in group classes.

It *is* possible to teach RMM to individual students. A teacher can make lessons fun and stress-free, and recitals can be voluntary. But the magic of the group dynamic—the friendship, mutual encouragement and positive influence of many peers—is missing in private instruction. Some adults can't (or won't) continue playing without the joy of the group. It is this social element of RMM that can keep people making music for a lifetime.

From the teacher's standpoint, group lessons are more financially rewarding than individual lessons. A teacher can often earn 2–3 times more income teaching groups. This fact alone may convince many teachers to make RMM classes at least a part of their regular teaching schedule.

KEY PRINCIPLES

Since RMM is taught primarily in groups, one would expect that any book on RMM teaching would contain an abundance of information on group teaching. This handbook, however, will not attempt to provide a thorough discourse on this topic. The authors recognize that there are numerous books already in publication that do an excellent job explaining the virtues and mechanics of the group approach. Two such publications are *Practical Piano Pedagogy*[1] and *Professional Piano Teaching*[2].

These respected sources will provide much more detailed information about group teaching and lesson planning than will be contained in this volume. However, there are some general group teaching principles that should be kept in mind by every RMM teacher.

---

1 Dr. Martha Baker-Jordan, *Practical Piano Pedagogy: The Definitive Text for Piano Teachers and Pedagogy Students* (Miami: Warner Bros., 2003), 83–97, 269–290.
2 Jeanine M. Jacobson, *Professional Piano Teaching: A Comprehensive Piano Pedagogy Textbook for Teaching Elementary-Level Students,* ed. E. L. Lancaster (Los Angeles: Alfred, 2006), 107–126, 206–210, 267–296.

Don't Be Wary When Skill Levels Vary

Even if all students in a beginning class appear to start at the same skill level, don't expect the class to stay that way. Some will grasp concepts quickly and others won't. The teacher should not be troubled by this diversity of skills. Regularly remind the class of the following:

- Learning to play the piano is a *process,* not a race. The goal is to enjoy the process.
- The "train of knowledge" leaves the station during the first class. But no one will be left behind if classes are attended regularly and practice is kept up at home.

Over time, the teacher may be surprised by the desire of the class members to stay together in their skill level. The influence of peers is a powerful motivator, even among adults. As slower-moving students observe the progress of other class members, many will be inspired to increase their home practice time to keep pace with the group. Also, faster-learners may provide assistance to slower students. As a result, the skill levels of class members can become less diverse over the course of a session.

Assign More to Those Who Soar

Despite the power of the group dynamic discussed above, a teacher may still be concerned about having bored achievers and struggling underachievers in the same class. This disparity can be addressed by varying home assignments. Though all class members learn the same concepts each week, one student may be given a "hands alone" assignment while a faster learner might be instructed to practice hands together or asked to play the right hand as written and create a *different* left hand part. Use creativity to keep the achievers appropriately engaged. Some fast learners may even enjoy serving as a teacher's assistant to help others.

Throughout the 8-week course session, encourage students to focus on their own individual progress rather than compare themselves to others. They will compare anyway, but this continual reminder will help alleviate stress and keep the class fun.

Let the Group Be a Group

Avoid the temptation to turn a group class into a room full of individual lessons. If that happens, all the valuable benefits of the group dynamic will be lost. RMM teachers should strive to keep class members engaged together in all activities during a class.

Sometimes it is helpful to have the class gather around one piano, allowing the teacher to demonstrate concepts, technique, or practice tips in a more intimate way. During such moments, encourage students to offer observations or opinions, or demonstrate an element that helped them improve. Open discussion in a group setting is always beneficial. Other ways to achieve optimum participation will be addressed later in this chapter.

Hear, Do, See, Discuss

The tendency in traditional teaching is to show a concept on the printed page and immediately assign a technical label to the concept. When teaching a concept such as directional (intervallic) reading, RMM students will learn more effectively when a teacher follows this sequence.

1. **Hear**—Hearing provides the best first exposure to a new concept. Let the group absorb the sound, the sensation and the description of the concept.

   Example:
   Play a series of repeated notes, steps and skips. Ask the class to describe the differences they hear between these examples. Before seeing the examples on paper or knowing any labels, students can usually discern that some sounds stay the same, others sound close together and others sound farther apart.

2. **Do**—Engage students in activities that help them develop coordination and muscle memory.

   Example:
   Ask students to play one key several times. Then, ask them to play two keys that are adjacent to each other. Lastly, ask them to play two keys that skip a piano key between them. (Do this with the white piano keys.)

3. **See**—Have students look at the concept or piece of music on paper.

   Example:
   On the grand staff, point out notes that are repeated, notes that are one-step apart and others that skip up or down in thirds. All piano methods have pages that illustrate these basic concepts.

4. **Discuss**—Give names or labels to the concepts without being too technical. Then, discuss how the printed notes relate to the sounds played by the teacher. Keep things simple—avoid too much information.

   Example:
   Use labels such as "steps" and "skips" to describe the notes heard and seen. These labels are easier to understand than intervals of seconds and thirds.

Using the *Hear, Do, See, Discuss* methodology will keep students engaged and increase their understanding of foundational concepts that occur in early classes.

Pacing, Not Racing

One of the most valuable skills a group teacher must learn is how to pace the class appropriately to avoid teaching to only the fastest or slowest students. The "train of knowledge" should always keep moving forward, but the train can slow down or speed up as needed. The teacher's goal should not be to complete the day's lesson plan but, rather, *to keep everyone in the class engaged*. Participation will determine the proper pace. There are several ways to know whether class members are fully engaged:

- Ask class members whether the pace is comfortable. They will usually speak up with an opinion if the pace is too fast or slow.

- Read the body language of the students. Sometimes class members will *say* the pace is comfortable when it really isn't. This happens when people are reluctant to admit they are struggling or too polite to admit they are bored. Scan the class continually for signs of struggle or fatigue, as well as frowns, quizzical looks, and glazed or wandering eyes.

Adults are better at masking emotions than children. But the vigilant teacher should still be able to see when members of the class have disengaged. When the above signs appear, do the following:

- Ask again if the pace is okay. Without identifying any individual, smile and say something similar to, "Your mouths are saying one thing, but your faces are saying another. Are we moving at the right pace?"

- Take an activity break. Pause the class for a moment and conduct a short, fun activity.

  Example:
  Have the group stand and make a circle with everyone facing in one direction along the circle. Then, have class members reach forward and massage the shoulders of the person in front of them. Laughter and smiles will follow.

A fun activity can re-engage the daydreamers and can sometimes give the teacher a moment to connect briefly with a slower-learner to see if any concept needs clarification.

There's No Practice Like Slow Practice

Always start with a slow tempo when the class plays together—especially when playing a piece for the first time. Slow practice is essential to allow the brain to process finger movements and concepts. When a tempo is too fast, students can become frustrated and discouraged. So, don't let the class rush. When students learn to practice slowly in class, they may remember to practice slowly at home. Let the classroom be a model for home practice.

Funny Is Money

Why did the RMM teacher cross the road? How many RMM students does it take to screw in a light bulb? What do you get when you throw a grand piano down a coal mine?

The punch lines aren't really important; although the answer to the last question—*A Flat Minor*—is worth mentioning. The point is that humor can be the RMM teacher's best friend. Students who enroll in RMM classes expect a fun, relaxed environment for learning. Humor keeps things loose. It can be as simple as reminding the students to keep a tip jar on their piano at home when they play for family or friends, or encouraging thunderous applause after a volunteer plays a simple piece during the first class. Help students laugh and play. It's healthy! Plus, it's good for business. When people enjoy RMM classes, they'll bring their friends, and classes will grow. So, when it comes to a teacher's revenue stream, funny is money.

By the way, how many RMM students does it take to screw in a light bulb? The best answer is...as many as it takes to make it fun! (Too bad that's not funny.)

The above principles apply to group teaching in any environment. The next two chapters will explore two different group environments and the teaching considerations that can help any RMM class be successful.

*RMM's best facilitators are NOT just talented musicians—
they are caring, compassionate and intuitive guides.*

—Karl Bruhn and Barry Bittman

Chapter 6 RMM TEACHING ON TWO PIANOS

Teachers who are unfamiliar with group teaching may automatically assume that it occurs only in a piano lab setting with multiple instruments (usually digital pianos). However, it may be a surprise to know that some of the profession's most influential teachers—the likes of Robert Pace and Richard Chronister—could teach group lessons on just *one* piano. Chronister once wrote, *"Students learn as a result of what and how they are taught, not as a result of how many students are in the room."*[1] That same wisdom applies to the number of instruments.

RMM classes can be taught with great success on two pianos sitting side-by-side. Many teachers using this format like the way it gives students opportunities to observe others and take notes. Others say it makes their classroom teaching easier, since students often focus more on the teacher than on the pianos. Once a teacher knows how to rotate the students at the pianos to ensure equal participation, classes of six or more can be easily taught with two pianos. This section will explain the step-by-step elements for success.

WIDE RANGE OF VENUES

Perhaps the greatest advantage of two-piano RMM teaching is the variety of sites where it can take place. Any location that can hold two instruments and enough chairs for class members is a viable venue. Options include the teacher's home studio, places of worship, senior centers, retirement communities and recreation centers. Even when music stores and colleges have piano labs, these locations can still be appropriate venues for two-piano teaching if this method is better suited to the needs of class members.

If an ideal location has only one piano, the teacher should contact a local piano retailer to explore loan, rental or purchase possibilities for the additional instrument, as discussed in Chapter 3. Remember that piano retailers will usually be quite happy to support any RMM teacher who has demonstrated the desire, ability and vision to create and retain new music makers.

INSTRUMENTS

When teaching with two pianos, there are three possible configurations:

- Two acoustic pianos.
- Two digital pianos.
- One acoustic piano and one digital piano.

The third configuration (one of each type) is optimal because it gives students playing experience on both types of instruments.

---

1 Richard Chronister, "The Irrelevant Controversy: Group Teaching vs. Private Teaching," *Keyboard Arts* (Spring 1992), 17.

Using Accompaniments

Pre-arranged accompaniments can add enjoyment and excitement to any RMM class. Accompaniments help to simulate the experience of playing with a larger ensemble— sometimes even a full orchestra. Many RMM teachers cannot imagine teaching a class without them.

When MIDI accompaniments are used, at least one digital piano is essential. Not only will the digital piano allow the teacher to mute tracks and adjust tempos, but it will also stay in tune with the accompaniments at all times. The ability to slow down accompaniments is extremely valuable for RMM teaching, especially with beginning classes where slow practice is encouraged.

When a class is taught with two *acoustic* pianos, MIDI accompaniments can still be played through a portable "MIDI Audio Player" that plays the accompaniments through audio speakers. This type of equipment offers the basic sound-generating features of a digital piano without the keyboard and large cabinet. Contact a local music retailer for more information about devices that offer this capability.

When a class is taught with two acoustic pianos and no MIDI Audio Player is available, the teacher can utilize "CD audio accompaniments" played through a portable stereo system. CD accompaniments offer the same class benefits as MIDI accompaniments, but do have disadvantages. No track or tempo changes are possible, and the pianos *must* be in tune with the CD. For these reasons, a configuration with at least one digital piano (allowing the use of MIDI accompaniments) is highly recommended.

CLASS SETUP FOR TWO-PIANO TEACHING

To set up a class for two-piano teaching:

- Place six or more chairs in a semi-circle facing the two pianos.
- Use a music stand with every two chairs.
- It is quite helpful, though not essential, for each student to have a small plastic replica of a piano keyboard (which can be obtained from a local music store). Such keyboards allow class members to try a concept when they are observing away from the piano. The keyboards provide the tactile sensation of playing and help to build confidence prior to each student's turn on the pianos.

MAXIMUM ENGAGEMENT

As stated earlier, keeping class members engaged in all activities is of paramount importance in two-piano RMM teaching. Depending on the concept being taught, there can be one, two or even three students sitting (or standing) at each of the pianos. Most of the time, however, there will be some students who observe, away from the instruments. Below are some ways to keep students engaged.

1. Introduce a new piece by playing it for the class (or listening to a recording) before anyone sees the music. Then, ask questions about the music that seem appropriate for the skill level of the class. Examples of questions for a beginning class might be:

   - Is the music fast or slow?

   - Is it loud or soft?

   - How did it make you feel? Why?

2. Later, ask students to look at the music and compare what they *see* on the page with what they *hear*. Discuss these observations together as a group. Questions to stimulate discussion might be:

   - Do hands play together or alone?

   - Which fingers are used for specific piano keys?

   - How does the player know how fast this piece should go?

   - Does the music "look" the way it sounds?

   Such questions will stimulate group dialogue that allows all class members to participate. This can also be an appropriate time to introduce basic musical vocabulary (e.g. *forte* means loud, *piano* means soft). Avoid the temptation to introduce too much theory. Keep things simple.

3. Demonstrate a concept using the plastic keyboard replica. Then, ask students to repeat that concept on their plastic keyboards. This "see and do" step keeps everyone involved. If plastic keyboards are not available, the teacher can show finger movements with one hand in the air and ask students to mimic those movements. Another way is to ask students to imagine a keyboard on their laps and perform the finger movements on the imaginary keyboard.

4. When students are asked to move to the pianos in groups of two or three (depending on the concept or the piece being taught[1]), any remaining students should practice the same music on their plastic keyboards (or on their laps). Alternatively, observing students can count aloud, name notes or engage in other appropriate activities while they watch the others play. Rotate positions so that all the students get an opportunity to sit at the pianos.

---

1 Simple concepts, such as playing quarter notes on one key, can be done with three students standing at each piano. A concept involving several notes played across multiple octaves might permit only two students at each piano. Two-hand concepts might allow only one student at each piano.

5. When a class member volunteers to play a solo, there are several inventive ways to keep the rest of the class engaged during the performance:

   • Before the volunteer plays, have class members listen to the assigned piece again and discuss what elements in the piece they found most challenging and interesting while practicing at home. This gives the volunteer soloist an opportunity to hear the piece and get some helpful perspectives before playing. The discussion also prepares the rest of the class to listen attentively to the elements discussed.

   • Ask the listeners to raise their hands every time the soloist plays a specified rhythm (such as a whole note). This listening game will sharpen the aural skills of fellow students and keep them engaged during the solo. It also reduces pressure on the soloist by shifting the focus from the performance to the game. As the class becomes more advanced, students can be asked to raise their hands for more complicated rhythms, chords or other musical elements.

   • Another approach is to have class members close their eyes while a student is playing. Ask listeners to raise their hands if they hear an incorrect rhythm or note. Be certain that neither the soloist nor the listeners can see the raised hands, as this is a diagnostic tool for the teacher only. This activity must be done with great sensitivity to ensure that it doesn't become a negative experience for any class member. Later, when class members are more comfortable with each other, the teacher can ask for this information verbally after a solo is completed.

   • When the volunteer is finished, ask the listeners to discuss what they enjoyed most about the soloist's playing. Then, ask the performer what he/she enjoyed about learning the piece and what improvements could be made.

Two piano teaching may be the approach used most by independent RMM teachers because it adapts easily to so many situations and venues. Some teachers, however, may have a relationship with a college or music retailer that puts a piano lab at their disposal. Chapter 7 will discuss ideas that can help teachers make the most of this opportunity.

"RMM teaching has influenced my traditional teaching. It has caused me to realize that helping people enjoy making music is in itself a worthy goal and will more likely keep students playing piano throughout their lifetime."

—RMM Teacher

Chapter 7 RMM TEACHING WITH A PIANO LAB

A piano lab offers many benefits to the RMM teacher:

- Every student can sit at a piano individually.
- Ensemble playing is possible anytime.
- MIDI accompaniments can be utilized on any instrument.
- The pianos will always be in tune with each other.
- Headphones allow periods when all students can practice alone.

Unfortunately, relatively few venues have piano labs. Independent teachers will often lack the physical space or financial resources to justify a lab. Retirement communities, senior centers and churches, known for their multi-faceted programs, are often reluctant to dedicate permanent space for a large installation of musical instruments. That leaves music stores, private music schools and colleges as the primary venues where piano labs can be found.

Still, many teachers regard group teaching with a piano lab as the best possible environment for RMM classes. They enjoy the technology, the various instrumental sounds, the ability to create an ensemble with lush layers, and the ability to have moments of silence even when everyone is playing simultaneously (through the magic of headphones).

The group teaching principles outlined in Chapter 5 (and the cited texts) provide a good foundation for RMM teaching in this setting. Therefore, this chapter will only highlight a few additional ideas to help students and teachers have fun in a lab situation:

Team Learning

Divide the class into two teams that share responsibilities for playing a piece. Assign roles in the following ways as a piece is played:

1. Let "Team A" be responsible for the right hand, while "Team B" plays the left hand.
2. Ask the teams to alternate playing measures (Team A plays measure 1, Team B plays measure 2, Team A plays measure 3, etc.)
3. Let team A count aloud while Team B plays hands together. Then, switch roles.
4. Rotate responsibilities so that everyone has an opportunity to experience all roles.

Class members will have fun working together to learn a piece—one element at a time. Once everyone is comfortable, have the entire class play the piece in unison.

Listen and Repeat

Evaluate aural skills with this listening game:

1. Play a very simple melody and ask students to echo what they hear (sing first, then play).
2. If students struggle, ask students to put on headphones and experiment to find the melody.

3. Go around the class and let each student play the melody.

4. If necessary, keep simplifying the melody until everyone experiences success.

Ensemble Playing

Turn any piece of solo music into an ensemble piece by dividing it into separate parts that are played with different orchestral sounds. For example:

1. Have one student play the bottom note in the bass clef with a double-bass sound.

2. Another plays the entire left hand part with soft strings.

3. Another plays the right hand part with a piano or electric piano sound.

4. Another plays the top treble clef note with a flute sound.

Ensemble playing is valuable for *any* player, not just RMM students. It develops students' listening, counting and collaborative skills. It also allows the class to study the character of various instrumental sounds. Take time to discuss why certain timbres are better suited for the treble or bass clef parts. Give the class time to experiment with different sounds.

There is also a wide array of music published for piano ensembles. The composers and arrangers of such pieces usually suggest specific sounds for each part. Classes can use the assigned sounds as a starting point and then experiment with other sounds.

A Note Regarding Traditional Students

Teachers who wonder whether their traditional students might enjoy the RMM approach will find ensemble playing to be the perfect way to introduce such students to RMM. Individual practice and performance are often solitary experiences for traditional students. Also, students who always play alone can develop bad habits, such as stopping after making a mistake, or slowing the tempo through difficult passages and rushing through easier ones.

For these reasons, ensemble playing can be both exhilarating and enlightening for traditional students, offering them the chance to interact with other players, enhance their listening skills (for maintaining steady tempo and balanced dynamics) and exercise creativity in the use of sounds, melody and rhythm. Other aspects of RMM—learning to play popular songs, understanding chords and lead sheets, and experimenting with improvisation in a group setting—may also be exciting to students who have not experienced these activities before. RMM may rejuvenate their love for the piano!

Quick Practice During Class

Some musical concepts are best learned when they are practiced immediately after they are explained. Piano labs allow this to happen in a group setting without the resulting cacophony of trial-and-error playing that can cause stress for some students. (Some people prefer to make their mistakes privately.)

After explaining the concept, ask students to practice with headphones for a minute or two. The teacher can walk around the room scanning for expressions of confusion or frustration. These contortions alert the teacher that a moment of clarification or encouragement is needed. When the headphones come off, the class should play the concept together. To make this more fun, ask students to play the concept (as a group) the way they did *before* the short practice session. If it sounds bad, enjoy a good laugh together. Then, play the "new and improved" version to hear the benefits of a few minutes of practice.

Using Special Sounds and Styles

Many digital pianos have special effects sounds (car horn, thunder, applause, footsteps, etc.) and superb rhythmic accompaniments that cover a diverse range of styles (swing, country, salsa, waltz, etc.). Use these features to create fun for the class!

Use the applause sound on high volume after someone volunteers to play a solo.

Find sounds that match a song title and insert them to generate a good laugh. For example, use a "dog barking" sound (if available) with "(How Much Is) That Doggie in the Window" or on the echo beats of "Blue Danube Waltz." Everyone in the class will want to take a turn making the dog bark.

After the class has become accustomed to certain CD or MIDI accompaniments, try replacing the background with a slightly different—or completely different—style. For example, try playing "When the Saints Go Marching In" as a polka (which is slightly different from the traditional March style) or as a salsa or country piece. Hilarity may ensue. But it will be good for the soul—and for the class.

A Reminder—Let the Group Be a Group

As mentioned in Chapter 5, the temptation in any group class—especially in a piano lab setting—is to create a room full of individual lessons. The convenience of headset communication and privacy makes it easy to slide into one-on-one interaction. Here are some suggestions to keep this from happening:

- Limit headset usage to only a few minutes at a time. When finished with headsets, immediately return to audible playing as a group.

- Rather than coaching students individually, ask the class to gather around the instructor's piano for a demonstration played by the teacher or a student. This method is particularly beneficial when it provokes questions from class members that can be answered by other students. Peer teaching is healthy for the group. As class members learn from student demonstrations and answer the questions of their peers, the group gains confidence and learns to progress on its own.

- Use MIDI accompaniments to keep the group focused. Start an accompaniment and direct the class to play along in unison. As the class plays, the teacher can stroll around the room to observe technical elements (hand position, posture, etc.), mastery of the concept, and, most importantly, whether students are enjoying the process.

Preparing for Success

Whether a teacher uses two pianos or a complete piano lab, one preparatory element that can help to ensure success in any environment is a well-crafted lesson plan. Chapter 8 will offer some valuable advice for RMM lesson planning.

"RMM teaching has helped me to relax a bit with my traditional teaching. It has allowed me to be more concerned with the students' goals and to be less uptight about measuring up to some artificial standard as a teacher."

—RMM Teacher

Chapter 8 LESSON PLANNING

There is something intrinsically oxymoronic about the idea of "RMM Lesson Plans." The concept is akin to assigning an important project to a colleague by saying, "Please take your time with this. There is *absolutely no rush*. I want it done by 10:00 A.M."

Lesson plans *do* provide valuable protocols for daily class content. But, by their very nature, they encourage accomplishment of specific goals within a defined period of time. Quite unintentionally, they can perpetuate the achievement mentality.

With this in mind, one could make a cogent case for the exclusion of formal lesson plans from any RMM curriculum. On the other hand, RMM teachers (particularly new ones) could benefit greatly from step-by-step plans that lead them through the teaching process. So, what should an RMM teacher do? To address this conundrum, the authors offer the following axiom:

"Plan to direct the class. Then, let the class direct the plan."

Lesson plans should never take the lead in an RMM situation. Certainly, the teacher should plan well for each lesson. But the actual amount of material covered during the lesson should depend solely on the comfort level of class members. In other words:

- *Be Patient*—Never move to a new concept until the group is truly ready.
- *Be Attentive*—Watch and listen for signs that indicate whether the group is confused or ready to move on.
- *Be Flexible*—Never forfeit fun and enjoyment for the sake of the lesson plan.

It may take two or even three lessons for some groups to cover the material contained in a typical one-day lesson plan. Other groups may progress much faster than expected. The key is to let the *students* establish the pace. There is *absolutely no rush*. Let the barometer of success be student enjoyment rather than musical accomplishment.

GUIDELINES FOR LESSON PLANNING

Many private piano teachers develop lesson plans for individual student lessons. However, sometimes such plans only involve turning pages in a method book. The student plays, the teacher listens and critiques—and the page is turned. That strategy won't be effective in a group setting.

Groups learn best when well-planned activities are used to ignite the group dynamic and engage students in fun, experiential learning. The best RMM lesson plans are both specific and creative; they list the steps of each activity clearly and concisely. Because group teaching requires maximum flexibility, it is wise to condense the steps of the lesson into a brief outline before the lesson begins. The use of an outline will keep things focused on the *concepts* rather than the details. Then, the teaching process is less likely to become rigid, and more likely to flow at a pace appropriate for the class. The components of a weekly RMM lesson plan should include:

- A list of general concepts that could be introduced during the class.
- A review of concepts/activities presented the previous week.
- A list of the strategies/activities used to demonstrate each new concept.
- Use of the *Hear, Do, See, Discuss* method first.
- A brief description of the steps of each activity.
- A summary of what the students have learned during the class.
- A description of the assignment for the following week.

Amid these elements, be sure to allow extra time for questions, feedback, class discussion and voluntary solos.

SAMPLE BEGINNER LESSON PLAN

The following is an example of a lesson plan from *Piano for Fun and Fulfillment*,[1] a curriculum that is taught with two pianos. This plan is written for week two of an eight-week session. It is written in outline form.

I. **Week Two Concepts**
   a. The Musical Alphabet
   b. Middle C
   c. White Piano Key Names

II. **Concepts from the Previous Week**
   a. Keyboard Geography
   b. Black Key Clusters
   c. Finger Numbers
   d. Sitting Position
   e. Hand Position

III. **Class Elements**
   a. **Review**
      i. Ask review questions that revisit the concepts from the previous week.
      ii. Ask for volunteers to play one of the three assigned pieces.
      iii. Ask for volunteers to play the black key "for fun" melodies.
   b. **Teach the musical alphabet**
      i. Go forward and backward with up and down hand gestures in the air.
      ii. Play the alphabet on the piano and ask the class whether the sounds go up or down.
   c. **Teach middle C**
      i. Note proximity to piano's brand name.
      ii. Call it "Navel C" if the player is sitting in front of the brand name.
      iii. Have the class find the remaining C's on the piano.

1 Brenda Dillon, *Piano for Fun and Fulfillment*, 2009.

   d. Teach the white key names

      i. Have the class play the white keys forward and backward on the piano while naming them aloud.

   e. Teach individual white piano keys with this chant:

      C is to the left of the two black keys

      D is in the middle of the two black keys

      E is to the right of the two black keys

      F is to the left of the three black keys

      G is in the middle of the three black keys

      A is in the middle of the three black keys

      B is to the right of the three black keys

      Now we're back to C.

   f. Use the MIDI accompaniment of "White Key Chant"

      i. Listen to the accompaniment and have the class sing names of the white piano key at the beginning of each line.

      ii. Rotate students at the pianos and have them play "White Key Chant" with the accompaniment.

   g. Teach the "Alphabet Waltz"

      i. Play the student part of "Alphabet Waltz" and have the class make hand gestures in the air as they hear the melody moving higher or lower.

      ii. Ask students if the melody was played in "steady, even sounds" or whether some piano keys were held longer (avoid technical terms at this point).

      iii. Have the class look at "Alphabet Waltz" (page 9).

      iv. Explain that the white circle notes are held longer than the black circle notes.

      v. Have students "talk" the song by saying: A (hold) B, C (hold) D...

      vi. Play "Alphabet Waltz" without accompaniment first; then with accompaniment.

      vii. Rotate students at the pianos.

      viii. Students sitting away from the pianos should simulate playing in the air and counting aloud (A (hold) B, C (hold) D...)

   h. Teach "Restless Theme"

      i. Hold up the pointer fingers of both hands and chant:

      E (hold)   E (hold)   E (hold)   E (hold)

      Right   Left   Right   Left

      ii. Have the class echo this chant while playing in the air.

      iii. Have students move down the alphabet with the same talking pattern for each letter name.

      iv. Have the class look at "Restless Theme" (page 10).

v. Ask the class to play it in the air while "talking" the letter names and slowly moving to the left.

vi. Rotate students (two at each piano) and play "Restless Theme" without accompaniment first, then with accompaniment.

i. Review concepts learned in this class

j. Assignments

i. Assign page 11, including review questions.

ii. Let students choose one or more of the songs for home practice.

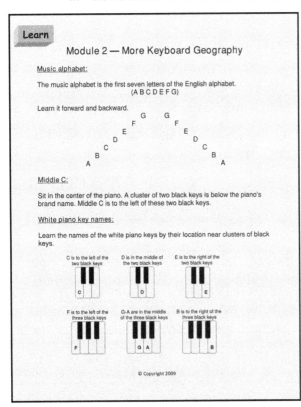

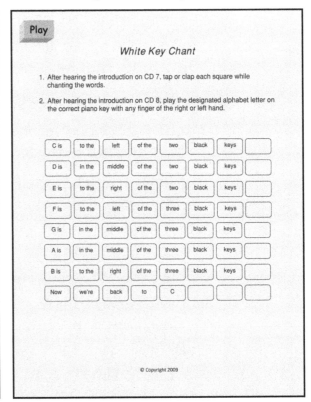

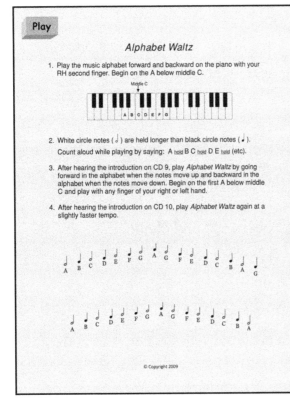

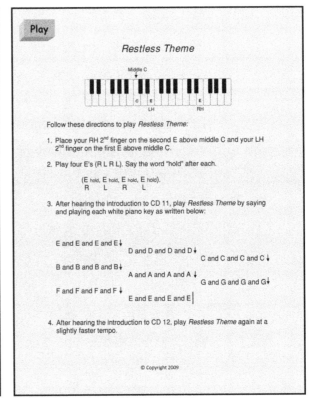

SAMPLE INTERMEDIATE LESSON PLAN

To provide a contrast to the previous beginner lesson plan, this example is designed for an intermediate-level class. Once again, the format is a class of six students using two pianos.

I. **Today's Concepts**

    a. G major scale (root position), close position (inverted) chords and arpeggios

    b. Harmonization: "At Last"

    c. Analyze "Polovetsian Dance" (arranged by Dennis Alexander)

II. **Previous concepts**

    a. Scale formula and fingering

    b. Root position and close position chords built on scale tones (I, IV, V)

    c. Harmonization of folk songs

    d. Analysis skills leading to quicker learning of repertoire

III. **Books**

    a. *Especially for Adults* (Book 1)—Dennis Alexander (Alfred)

    b. *Not Just Another Scale Book*—Mike Springer (Alfred)

    c. Lead Sheet—"At Last"

IV. **Class Elements**

    a. Review—Hear volunteers play scale and chord assignment, folk tune harmonization and assigned repertoire.

    b. Teach the G major scale

        i. Discuss scale formula and fingering for G major scale.

        ii. Rotate the class at the pianos to play the scale—hands separately or together

    c. Teach "At Last"

        i. Discuss LH chords and harmony.

        ii. Have one student play RH melody while another plays block LH chords.

        iii. Rotate the class at the pianos.

    d. Teach "Polovetsian Dance"

        i. Play "Polovetsian Dance" for the class.

        ii. Ask discussion questions:

           • What is the key of the piece?

           • How many measures are in the introduction?

           • If the melody (theme) begins on measure 5, on which measure does it repeat?

        iii. Determine the measure numbers for the following:

           • Intro (measures 1–4)

           • Theme (measure 5 through first beat of measure 12)

           • Repetition of theme (measure 12 through first beat of measure 19)

           • Closing (measures 19–26)

iv. Rotate the class at the pianos. While one student plays the RH melody, another should play and name the LH intervals of measures 1–4 and 19–26 (fifths and sixths)

v. Analyze the chords of measures 5–11 (C, D7, G, Em, Am, D and G). Have the class write correct alphabet letter above each measure as it would appear on a lead sheet.

vi. Discuss fingering of RH melody on measures 5–11. Observe cross-over fingerings and circle finger substitutions.

e. Review the concepts learned in this class

f. Assignments

i. Play "Polovetsian Dance" (hands separately or hands together *slowly*), measures 1 through first beat of measure 12.

ii. Play "Red River Valley," RH melody and blocked or broken LH chords on first verse.

iii. G major scale, root and close position chords and arpeggio.

SUMMARY

The sample lesson plans provided in this chapter are detailed and well organized. Any teacher who plans with such care will certainly be prepared to teach an RMM class. But the skilled group teacher never forgets the prime directive of RMM lesson planning:

"Plan to direct the class. Then, let the class direct the plan."

Be prepared to teach well. Then, relax and have fun!

"RMM classes are absolutely crucial to the future of our industry."
—RMM Retailer

Chapter 9 PARTNERING WITH RETAILERS

Chapter 3 described ways that teachers can partner with piano retailers when RMM classes are taught *outside* a retail store. This chapter will examine the natural alternative: partnering with a retailer to create an RMM program *inside* a music store. It will rely upon the insights of active RMM retailers in providing answers to the following questions:

- What do retailers think about RMM?
- What do retailers see as their greatest challenge in establishing RMM classes?
- What traits are retailers looking for in an RMM teacher for their store?
- How is compensation determined for in-store teaching?
- What resources can a retailer provide to assist the RMM teacher?

THE RETAILER PERSPECTIVE

Four successful piano retailers were invited to provide their perspectives on in-store RMM teaching. The participants were:

- Bill Dollarhide, Dollarhide's Music Center (Pensacola, FL)
- Christi Foster and Deborah Story Carter, Foster Family Music (Bettendorf, IA)
- Robert Scott Richardson, Reifsnyder's (Lancaster and Mechanicsburg, PA)
- Wayne Reinhardt, Schmitt Music Company (Minneapolis, MN)

All of these retailers were early adopters of the RMM concept. The following information is based upon their comments and experiences.

What do retailers think about RMM?

Not all piano retailers have music education programs. But the savvy ones understand that education is vital to their existence. Specifically, they see RMM teaching as the critical link to a huge segment of the population (adult learners) that has been underserved by the musical community.

One member of the retailer panel, Robert Scott Richardson, commented, "RMM classes are absolutely crucial to the future of our industry. Obviously, I want to sell pianos, but RMM is bigger than that. As I've talked to students and have seen their excitement, I've learned that my 'home run' is seeing students who are genuinely happy about playing the piano. As they enjoy music making, they become our friends…and, eventually, they become our customers."

Christi Foster of Foster Family Music said, "It would be fairly quiet in our stores without a thriving lesson program. Because of the RMM classes, students come in early. We have the opportunity to socialize and get to know them. Our goal is for our teachers and sales staff to become trusted experts and advisors to our students. The increased store traffic from in-store lessons has not only increased sales, but also the awareness of our store in the community as RMM classes have generated a buzz with the local press."

These types of comments are quite common among retailers who have experienced the tremendous benefits of RMM teaching in their stores. But not all retailers have been similarly enlightened. Many still need to be cajoled—by their industry peers and by teachers—to join the ranks of RMM devotees.

In making the case for RMM to a retailer, teachers should be supremely confident that their efforts will help bring prosperity to any retailer. Never be discouraged if the storeowner shows little interest. Just try another retailer. The smart ones will listen carefully to what you have to say.

What do retailers see as their greatest challenge in establishing RMM classes?

The retailers responded in vigorous unison to this question. Their answer was *"finding the right teacher."* Retailers are adamant that a teacher must *fully* embrace the RMM philosophy in order to succeed. The principles of having fun, learning without stress and nurturing the *whole* person cannot be compromised. In their collective experience, they have observed teachers who attempted to apply traditional performance-based techniques to RMM—only to fail. Therefore, retailers take great care to select teachers who embody the RMM philosophy and represent the right fit for their organization.

What traits are retailers looking for in an RMM teacher for their store?

Responses to this question had little to do with a teacher's level of education or prior training in piano pedagogy. In fact, some retailers admitted to being "somewhat wary" of teachers with a long history of traditional teaching experience—fearing that such teachers might be unwilling or unable to make the transition to RMM.

Retailers said they were looking for a type of *person* rather than a type of *teacher*. The following words were used to describe the ideal candidate:

- Upbeat
- Energetic
- Positive
- Relaxed
- Friendly
- Caring
- Empathetic
- Organized
- Possessing a great attitude

The experience of retailers has shown that teachers with these personal traits, regardless of educational background, have the best chance of succeeding as an in-store RMM teacher.

One additional trait of an ideal candidate is the "willingness and ability to foster positive and trustworthy relationships between the sales staff and RMM students." An RMM teacher does not need to become a salesperson, but should at least become an ardent facilitator of healthy relationships that can lead to a sale. The RMM teacher who is able to skillfully connect the dots between salespeople and students to increase store sales will be a hero to the storeowner.

Keep in mind that just as teachers rely on paying students to continue teaching, retail stores rely on serious customers to stay in business. If the existence of a local music store provides real *value* to a community, a supportive RMM teacher will be serving that community by creating active music makers who become store customers.

How is compensation determined for in-store teaching?

Teacher compensation plans may vary widely from one retailer to another. Some already have a traditional teaching program and will base teacher compensation on the structure of their existing program. Others may let the teacher establish class tuition separately and will simply charge a flat "facility fee" for the use of their teaching areas. Others may request a percentage or fixed dollar amount for each student.

Session fees should be comparable to fees charged for similar group lessons in the local community, unless the teacher and retailer decide to offer the beginner session at a special introductory rate to boost first-time enrollment.

If a teacher begins to discuss compensation with a retailer who has never before offered in-store lessons, the following tips may be helpful:

- Suggest a compensation plan to the storeowner (perhaps the "facility fee" concept or a fixed amount per student as described above). It is often easier and faster to initiate a compensation plan than to wait for a retailer to develop one. If the proposal meets with resistance, the teacher can always work with the retailer to develop an alternative plan that is mutually acceptable.
- Determine in advance *how* student fees will be paid. That is, will class fees be paid to the store or to the teacher?
- Put the parameters of the compensation plan in writing to avoid misunderstandings.

What resources can a retailer provide to assist the RMM teacher?

A retailer can often provide a wide range of promotional support for an RMM program. This is one of the key added benefits of working with a retailer. Promotional support may include:

- Verbal promotion of RMM classes to all store customers.
- Direct mailing of letters and flyers to the community.
- In-store signs.
- Brochures and flyers (placed in senior centers, libraries, grocery stores).
- Telephone calls to customer prospects made by sales staff.
- Ads and announcements on the store website.
- Newspaper stories and advertisements.
- Radio promotion in connection with the store's regular ads.
- Ads and editorial content in senior publications and local township newsletters.
- "Kick-off events" (with demonstration lessons) to generate interest.
- Seminars that introduce the health benefits of music making.
- Periodic master classes with guest artists.
- Space for various types of piano celebration events (in place of recitals).

While few stores can provide *all* these support elements, a retailer relationship will normally generate far more visibility for an RMM program than could be achieved by an independent teacher working alone.

SUMMARY

As stated in Chapter 3, teachers and retailers can be excellent partners when both are focused on creating *more music makers*. History shows that RMM programs enjoy their greatest success when teachers and retailers are working together toward this goal.

CLOSING THOUGHTS

As a final exercise, think back on a time when someone tried to teach you a concept or a skill—but did it all wrong. Perhaps it was a high school teacher who went too fast and never stopped to ask if you understood the material; a driving instructor whose continual criticisms made you feel pressured and inadequate; a coach who told you to do something beyond your current capability and then belittled you for failing to do it well; or even a parent whose instructions were always accompanied by words and facial expressions conveying the impression that you, and your abilities, weren't good enough.

If you've had such experiences, can you recall how you felt at the time? Do words such as "discouraged," "angry" and "incompetent" come close to capturing the emotions? Like it or not, *millions of people are afraid to pursue music making today because they believe—correctly or incorrectly—that formal music instruction will leave them feeling that way.* They believe that they lack talent, and that this failing could invite the derision and disrespect of others. So, they never try.

You can change this reality.

Recreational Music Making was born to create a *revolution.* Not a revolution against traditional ways of teaching, but a revolution against the notion that music making is only for those with talent. RMM dares to declare that music making is for *everyone.* And it invites all those who have ever dreamed of playing a musical instrument— including the millions upon millions who wish they had never given up their piano lessons—to give us another chance.

For those of us who believe that a world filled with music makers will be a *better* world, this is the opportunity of a lifetime—our best chance to make a difference in a complicated, needy society. May this book provide some of the early chapters of what will one day be seen as an epic saga—a bigger-than-life musical narrative in which tens of millions were drawn to an art form that unleashed a remarkable renaissance of human flourishing, and brought joy and healing to all.

It all starts with a few welcoming, encouraging words to the dreamers:

"Come on in...

        it's safe in here...

                you *will* succeed...

                        we promise."

YOU CAN
PLAY THE PIANO

We Promise.

Want to play your all-time favorite songs?

Thought it was **too late** to learn to play?

Played **years ago** and want to try again?

A Recreational Music Making Class Is Your Answer.

Classes are taught in supportive groups and offer the following:

- A stress-free environment, beneficial to your health and well-being.
- An ideal setting for meeting new friends and having fun.
- A trained music instructor who will help you learn without frustration.

Contact us today to attend a *FREE* **Preview Lesson**
during the week of Month, Dates.

Your Music Studio
Phone; Email address; Website
Physical address and zip/postal code
Directions to studio

RECOMMENDED RESOURCES

DVDs

RMM Documentary DVD—This DVD includes testimonials from RMM students and teachers. It can be viewed on *YouTube*, as well as the National Piano Foundation website (http://www.pianonet.com), by clicking the tab marked *Recreational Music Making*, then the *RMM Documentary DVD* tab. The Documentary DVD is also available for purchase from the National Piano Foundation.

Recreational Music Making Four-DVD Set—This four-DVD set was filmed at the 2008 MTNA National Conference in Denver. It covers the following topics: *How to Get Started, How to Partner with Retailers, Three Different Paths to RMM Teaching, How Adults Learn, Teaching Ideas for Advanced Levels, Giving the Gift of Chords, Ensemble Playing* and *How to Integrate Traditional Piano Students in RMM classes.* The four-DVD set is available for purchase from the National Piano Foundation.

To view a short trailer, go to www.pianonet.com. Click the *Recreational Music Making* tab, then click *RMM DVDs Available for Purchase,* and finally, select *Click here to watch a trailer for the DVDs.*

Periodicals

Making Music (http://www.makingmusicmag.com)—A magazine for adult musicians with articles devoted to amateur music makers.

Clavier Companion (http://www.claviercompanion.com)—A magazine for piano teachers published bi-monthly. Includes several sections: *Inside the Profession, Home Practice, Jazz & Pop, Music Reading, Technique, Rhythm, Perspectives in Pedagogy, Adult Piano Study, Repertoire & Performance, Technology, News & Views* and *Keyboard Kids' Companion.*

American Music Teacher (http://www.mtna.org)—A magazine for teachers of piano, voice and other instruments. Published bi-monthly for MTNA members, it offers pedagogical articles, resource information, forums, and news about MTNA programs and members.

PianoNotes (http://www.pianonet.com)—A newsletter for members of the National Piano Foundation. Published quarterly, it includes numerous RMM articles.

RMM Handbook Articles

Austin, Karen and Austin-Allen, Toni. "Recreating Recreation." *PianoNotes* (Spring 2007): 1.

Cassaday, Barbara. "Recreational Music-Making—Piano Professionals Get Involved." *Piano Technicians Journal* (March 2007): 6.

Chung, Brian. "How to Change the Future of Music Making." Keynote speech for the World Piano Pedagogy Conference (October 27, 2006). Also on http://www.brianchung.net (February 1, 2009).

Chung, Brian and Dillon, Brenda. "Piano Teaching—Traditional or Recreational? What's the Difference?" *American Music Teacher* (October/November 2008): 46, 87.

Dillon, Brenda. "Create Excitement with Celebrations and RMM Players Clubs." *PianoNotes* (Winter 2008): 1–2.

Dillon, Brenda. "A Different Kind of Music Making." *American Music Teacher* (April/May 2008): 68.

Dillon, Brenda. "How Do You Incorporate RMM into Your Teaching?" *Keyboard Companion* (Autumn 2007): 32–35.

Dillon, Brenda. "Recreational Music Making—The Future of Music Teaching?" *American Music Teacher* (August/September 2007): 21–23.

Dillon, Brenda. "RMM—One Teacher's Journey." *PianoNotes* (Summer 2006): 1–3.

Dillon, Brenda. "Why Is Playing the Piano Important to Our Country?" *PianoNotes* (Winter 2009): 1, 3.

Dunn Williams, Amy. "Join the Club: Group Piano Lessons Offer a Relaxed and Fun Alternative to Traditional Teaching Methods." *Making Music* (March/April 2008): 8–10.

Geffen, Susan. "Recreational Music Making: One Educator's Perspective." *PianoNotes* (Fall 2007): 2–4.

Ingle, Gary. "Keyboard Pedagogy and the Future: Lessons from Human Genome Research: an Interview with Barry B. Bittman, M.D. and Karl T. Bruhn." *American Music Teacher* (October/November 2005): 4–9.

Johnson, Rebecca. "Take Two Music Lessons and Call Me in the Morning: An Interview with Karl Bruhn." *Keyboard Companion* (Summer 2007): 34–37.

Jutras, Peter and Dillon, Brenda. "Improving with Age: Current Trends in Adult Music Research and Teaching." *Abstracts: 28th ISME World Conference*, July 2008, 103–105.

Ledet, Andrew. "RMM Conversion." *Music Inc.,* January 2008, 16.

Perez, Debra. "Recreational Music Making (RMM.)" *Keyboard Companion,* Summer 2008, 35–36.

"PTG Offers Scholarship in Support of RMM." *Piano Technicians Journal* (November 2007): 38.

"PTG Supports Teachers through MTNA Scholarships." *Piano Technicians Journal,* (June 2008): 39.

Severson, Lara. "4 Ways a Recreational Perspective Boosted the Piano Segment." *PLAYback* (Winter 2009): 14.

Wanta, Charity. "It's Never Too Late—Learn to Play an Instrument as an Adult." *Wisconsin Woman* (December 2007): 34–35.

Websites

National Piano Foundation Website (http://www.pianonet.com)—Contains information about RMM seminars and DVD resources. Click the *Recreational Music Making* tab for RMM information. Click the *Group Piano Teacher* tab for information on group teaching.

NAMM Website for RMM (http://rmm.namm.org)—Contains information about RMM for piano and other instruments. Find articles and news in six sections: *News, Lifestyles, Community, Research, Learning Center* and *Facilitator Corner*. RMM piano teachers can submit information to be included in the Facilitator Corner.

American Music Conference RMM Site (http://www.amc-music.com/rmm/programs.htm)— Provides information on RMM philosophy, RMM benefits, research on music making, important web links and upcoming events.